Parallel Universes

Parallel Universes

Stephen M. Honig

Parallel Universes
ISBN: 979-8-218-36885-2

Author Photo Back Cover by Laura Unflat
Design & Production by Jennie Hefren
Editorial Direction by Howard Wells

Printed in the USA

This volume is dedicated to all poets fending off obsolescence at the hands of electronic successors.

FOREWORD

In August of 2023, the Paris Museum of Modern Art exhibited works by seven artists which were so unlike "modern art" as to suggest they were not of this world. The curator explained the exhibition in cosmological terms, in "a parallel world, defined as a universe with its own measure of space and time. If such worlds existed, they would logically have to be separate from our own and governed by different laws, thus overturning fundamental principles we have considered as absolute and unchangeable."

The canvases were highly abstract, stripped of all recognizable elements; varying seas of form, color and texture. How to look at these works? Visitors were invited to "broaden our usual modes of perception, generally anchored in the visible world, in order to transport us into a poetic and emotional parallel universe." We were told that these artists had established "precise rituals in order to connect with invisible forces."

This visitor was suspicious of the exhibition's basic premise. Given the wide scope of modern art, encompassing incredible differences in concept, media, execution and abstraction, could these works really be so different as to fall outside the canon?

Any definition of "modern art" also runs afoul of the dubious genesis of the entire concept of "modern art" itself. Roger Scruton ascribes the purpose of this invented category ("modern") to an effort to make art inaccessible to the average person. Prior art forms had been embraced by the hoi polloi, and thus debased and in need of rescue by the invention of a more obscure category known only to the artistically elite. Poetry in the age of the "modern" world had become too available, too understood, by the "wrong" people; "rhyme and metre had become the stuff of Christmas Cards."

Hence the need to invent a new, more stringent definition of art (art in a parallel world) which could be shared (at least for a while) only among those types who find themselves in Paris and feel compelled to "culture up" by going to a distant Metro stop to locate the Museum of Modern Art.

Perhaps the curator at the Paris Museum of Modern Art might have felt that same urge, experienced by those who named the current "modern canon," to salvage the works in his August show through a more arcane designation or category, and he hit upon the concept of art in a parallel universe.

What if the same standard of re-categorization were applied to poetry? What if a new poem was so divorced from its subject so as to not mention directly or even hint directly at the poem's subject in any way, either by description or clear inference? Would that poem then be so different in form from what presently is contained in the plethora of current poetical works, that it could be claimed to exist in a different, parallel universe?

Is there an experiment to test such poetic possibility? None existing, I invented the methodology below to explore the concept.

This volume is an effort to write poetry with the intent not to depict in any way the thing that is the poem's subject but, rather, just the emotional image that such original subject left in the mind of the poet, deposited on the page, otherwise untethered to its source. Does this create a "new" poetry falling into a new "universe"? Is it even poetry at all? Or, mere self-indulgence?

This "experiment" is doubly burdened, perhaps to the extent of certain failure. Not only does the poetry itself suffer from its initial premise, but also the entire effort is burdened with the limitations of this writer—a self-taught poet so busy with writing and with life that he may well lack the knowledge to engage the premise intelligently.

If the premise of a parallel universe is so dubious, and if this author is so limited, why then was this experiment even undertaken? This is the question posed to me by my vexed editor, himself a paragon of logic ever anxious to trim back my illusions. I was admonished to explain my intent to his satisfaction, for the benefit of the ultimate reader.

I confess that I did not have an immediate answer, and upon reflection remained confused as to my motive. And if I am confused, how can the reader take this volume seriously?

My conclusion is this: what if, indeed, the museum curator was not reaching in misguided intellectual folly, nor reaching for a "marketing hook" to induce public visitation to a rather varied collection of canvases.

Perhaps evolution of art had taken us to an opportunity to reexamine what we produce and, in so doing, reach a better intellectual understanding of what can be painted (or written)? The very naming of an evolving body of work feeds back into the mind of the creators, opening possibilities of thought not previously considered. Is this realization a benefit derived from the human drive to put everything into categories so as to heighten understanding?

I invite you to explore this collection, in light of the process of its creation, to see if the exercise suggests an enhanced level of understanding. Poetry is an exercise occurring over time, and has had numerous prior inflection points which have driven innovation. I do not presume to suggest that the poems have achieved that result, nor that the method of their creation is causal. That task is up to you.

+ +

I have a memory of a character in the movies, or perhaps appearing in early television, or even a radio character from a time when stories were told over commercial radio, who had the perfect prefix for this book. I confess that neither I nor my three oldest friends, each sharing my weight of years, could recall the name of this character; but my memory is clear that this character regularly tackled problems of great complexity and danger without hesitation.

This memory has provided me the courage to attempt this experiment in the throes of unwarranted confidence. I have written this book "UNDAUNTED BY THIS FOUL TURN OF EVENTS."

USER MANUAL

The following thirty poems are formatted as follows: on the facing page is a poem without a title; on the reverse side of that page is a title indicating the original subject (in terms of poetry, a "prompt").

Here are some questions to consider after reading these poems; the questions address whether a poem inhabits a new genre (we will call it a parallel universe) and if such poems can be conceived by purposeful use of the described methodology:

Did you guess the original subject from the poem itself?

Now that you see the title, do you get any sense of its original subject?

Is the poem to your mind successful on any level?

Does the poem fall within your current concept of modern poetry, or is there a difference you perceive as something, on balance, that is "new"?

Extra credit: once you have read all the poems, select a subject, wait a day or two, and then write a poem that is your best shot at fulfilling the experimental thesis of this book: emotionally derivative, without any express reference to the original subject matter, capturing for you the subject's essence in a new way, thus constituting the poem as a contender for the designation of "out of this world."

Lastly, please read the Afterword to this book, a personal anecdotal speculation on the nature of parallel universes suggested by an excellent article by Stephanie Burt in the November 7, 2022 issue of *The New Yorker*.

That article begins with a quote from a Jorge Luis Borges short story, which in turn recounts the story of a scholar who, by choosing from among all possible fictional narratives, by definition eliminates all other realities; thus, quoting Borges, "[h]e creates, in this way, diverse futures, diverse times which themselves also proliferate and fork."

If every time you write a poem you have implicitly contemplated and rejected every conceivable alternative version, then can you conclude that every poem, no matter the subject nor the process by which it was written, creates parallel universes by definition?

Poem #1

sloshing sox
drooping shoulders

ennui
      on me
          on all.

Cats in the alley, Brooklyn New York March 1956
garbage can cover clatters to the ground
a thousand gentle drummings

people stooped leaning into their strides

water comes up from the floor
      proof certain the world folding in on itself
         oozing upwards in the squeeze

damp shoulders shudder
monotone out the window
      brown the new gray.

A woman crying through the night
      through an open window
         through a pain she cannot understand
          cold chill through and through

I am so alone

Rainy Day

Poem #2

Not what I figured but

         then

what can one know until one knows,

know what I am saying?

You take it on faith and faithfully thusly you arrive

joined by many whose faith joins the faithful

and, for the moment, floats the promise

      before synapses fail.

In the Revolution, they say that heads winked as they rolled but

      the joke was funny only for an instant...

followed by the caskets of collaborateurs.

Advertising deceives

      as you only get frequent flier miles one way.

Heaven

Poem #3

clap your hands,

yeah you

'cause today is the day

to clap your hands

per the instruction sheet.

You do not seem convinced?

You expect proof?

YOU did not read the instructions.

It does not get delivered that way.

You need to unwrap it on your own.

Then we suggest you grab it by its tendrils and dig your

nails into it

because it is a slippery son of a bitch

always on the make for something new

       that does not involve you.

Happy

Poem #4

Merits on display

       desire desirous desired designed designated dedicated.

Is not the sun about to shine

& are we not to be shined upon?

Do you take a shining?

But   do you hear the rumor

            shards of evidence

that suns set and

      in the darkness..

         in the darkness!

            in the darkness?

I promise you the sun.

I promise (   )

Marry Me

Poem #5

winter in an instant

night without end

wind without sound

sound without content

fire to dust

dust to dust

      embraced inexplicably...

will it come to this for me, as seems

uncomputable

      un-understandable

        unprobable...

AAAAHHHHHHHHH

            saved forever in grace

or so it is said

Death Comes A-Visiting

Poem #6

not for me

no one asked

if only I could decide

      sense of promise but

         they have issued me a permit with no guarantees

and they think I do not understand

Birth

Poem #7

You pulse like in orgasm

flowing outward to infinite pleasures

reliant on no one

      until

      without notice

      your promise fades for all to see-

if they know where to look.

Stars

26

Poem #8

zazz jumble tumble

rock and roll

pixels rumble

and I awoke one day without my mind

what a relief to lie there eyes closed seeing

February 2023 NOLA with beads flying

music on parade in empty spaces filled

while listeners were either all of one hue

or all of none

Color

Poem #9

Float fall boom dream

Sometimes tied to a scream

Need it, read it

Captured, freed it

Alone, a crowd

A gown, a shroud

Stop it

Pop it

Hop it

Coming humming drumming slumming

She slid down and glowed from her lips

Music

Poem #10

Clean oiled shining long and strong

the old man rocked back and forth in the tall grass

dawn came silently across the plain

and, as life stirred,

the world fell down in blood and death

dogs baying at the sun

Shot Gun

32

Poem #11

Hello not stranger

Nor strange

But essence of life

Yet avoided evaded reviled derided

Pain unimaginably necessary in not-so-polite company

Blind eyes staring obliquely

Envy of freedom

Lack of cant

Folding textures riding waves of abject abandon

While, inside, someone sips tea with chocolates.

Why do I want to write longer about this,

Such distant titillation aimed at innocents

       ssssssssssssssssshhhhhhhhhhhhhhhhhh

Excrement on the Sidewalk

Poem #12

Hey good buddy/buddies

Protector/assailer

Cosmic sailor

Whatcha got on your mind this eon that I gotta duck dodge deal

But hell this is a big topic so set down a bit and wait........

Waiting for it

Suspicion for some

Vain for others

But the love the love the love

Borne on spires

Born on desires

—in Paris there is a basement full of discarded tombstones

       of people chosen

          by some metric.

Need AI to scrape the data from the sky.

Gods

Poem #13

Yes.

Mess.

G-d bless.

Hard to find

Blows my mind

Any time

Any kind.

Blue Danube Waltz

and somewhere Joshua's trumpet is playing taps...

Encore une fois je vais dans le bois

Sex

Poem #14

Layered secrets

Streaks of oil

Aroma of farmlands

Glistened

Trapped oblivion

Laughter at midnight

Soft soft soft

Tobacco and lead pencils abound...

Red Wine Glass

Poem #15

Rip the shit out of you if you look crosswise

And you deserve it.

Knots of fury

Glare of hatred

Power of a million years of pain

Shreds your sorry ass and you deserve it.

Safe now you think, but forever is a very long time.

Callooh callay and come galumping back...

So sad it is to be beautiful yet out of your space and time.

Zoo Tiger

Poem #16

Killer without remorse

Rare predator

Saucy and aloof

Red red red bleed for me, bleed because of me

Torn from grass and air

Subservient in the ultimate degree

You exist to serve yet

Your revenge even now is eating at so many hearts.

I kiss you without remorse.

Filet Mignon

Poem #17

There is blood on the land
blood on the hand
twisting, gripping rubbing shards of bone
All to ill use.
if not death now, then surely later   often
undeserved in the heart of the decedent
and for the holder, ahh yesssss
the thrill.

Absolved the felon, for a single thrust is pallid
infantile
invisible
in the eyes of Gods such as these
where sharp definitions do not lead to truth.

Knife

Poem #18

Green squander

Field of waste

Flowing on the currents of commerce

Facilitating sin in every crevice

None immune

Played on a game board empty of lines

     and the book of rules long lost.

Fold rolled sold bold hold gold

I saw you do it/ I know who you are

Guilt and not giving a shit being two different sides of the

coin.

     For two bits I'll fade to black...

     For two bits I'll fold...

     Ain't nuthin' I won't do for two bits...

Money

Poem #19

Floating free
Without air

Narrow worlds for narrowed minds

I hear voices of women
I hear the songs of birds
I can now hear all better than before

No context no contact no no no no no

NO

The Royal Canal

Prison

Poem #20

So there is darkness here that must be repressed

in the name of something without a name.

Not so much an idea as a suggestion.

Music in repressed corners mentioning chords of discontent

repressed by the fear

      that goddammit there is no tune.

Electronic music unheard is all I hear.

My Mind

Poem #21

One wrong word and I am destroyed.

He know, you know.

All sorts of things I do not wish to know.

If you know them, please do not mention them

       as I am a sensitive soul.

He makes cider from my adams apple

ground fine, soured and metastasized,

       refreshing if you are ready.....

—I know I am not being told about what those atoms are doing.

Doctor

54

Poem #22

Playing the ivories

white with black interstices

hiding rot to the core

sharp pains and the smoke of night plays tickling songs

I have a collection, the smaller kinds

lost by the wayside in the journey of life

and with little value

(embarrassed as it were by portentous drift)

...but then again, what does?

Teeth

Poem #23

I force unwilling axions to engage.

I fail, drooping from underload/overload

       into exhausted catharsis of guilt because of it.

It is a mirror and as such fails to please.

Glints of light distort true image.

Then again

       on the odd chance...

Religious Worship

58

Poem #24

Lusting after the ultimate con
inside buildings of vast grandeur.
There is something going on that I cannot understand.
You say you do, but I know you lie
or perhaps
it is mere delusion, so common
among those so afraid.

It is dark rot, rotting in the dark.

It is stark naked hubris
learned by those who learn nothing of the universe
as the lesson is the deterioration of knowledge into reality.

Someone once explained it thusly: XXXXXXXXXXXXX

Got it?

Beating to the meter, pulsing pulsing nonplussed nonpulsed
      non non non non
Non non non non non non non non non non non non non
      non non non non

In Brooklyn so very long ago a young girl asked
      the ultimate question of me:
"What part of 'no' do you not understand?"

I replied, "second letter confuses me."

Eternal Life

Poem #25

Purposely hidden by fire and time

silent of the past

without guidance for the future

we now presume

 to peel them open

for our own ends

idle curiosity its own reward

spurred by the ancient word

for purple...

Scrolls of Pompeii

In the Fall of 2023, science believed it found a way to read the scrolls burned by the heat of Vesuvius. Prior efforts at unrolling the scrolls rendered them dust. A way was found to read the scrolls while leaving them wound up and dark as coal. The first word discovered was ancient Greek for the color purple.

Poem #26

float cold into

rhythm

patter

winds askew

flowers die / onslaught

oozing slipping slithering

reality roars

reflecting off shining roadways

bundled

v's checkmarks on black macadam

you were there and then you were gone

Rain

Poem #27

?

memory promised memory denied

gods conspire

but
not for me

you did not care enough
or care to try

Death

Poem #28

iamb

lamb

spam

dram

scram

damn

BLOOD PRESSURE

DESIRE HIDDEN/DENIED

poor people ponder perpetually

i am vastly confounded

Poetry

Poem #29

curl
rot
itch

        worms splits blood cracks pain
            arctic blue
            blue hair

get a job

pota

ugly ugly ugly ugly

I saw you that night and looked down and you have never
been the same to me and you do not even know it

Toes

Poem #30

mirror

afloat

fear of rabbits

love of men

driven by pronouns

punch through the membrane

        show me
     death bodiless absolute ennui

hello Dali
"precise rituals in order to connect with invisible forces"

escape

escaping

escaped

     atoms
        electrons
          quarks
            dark matter
              universal
Linda Blair
Friedrich Nietzsche
              orgasm

Charlotte Rampling

Parallel World

AFTERWORD

This volume explores this basic "Question": whether there is such a thing as a parallel universe when it comes to the arts, and particularly poetry. The poetry in this book is an attempt to explore the possibility that poetry can be written today that falls so far outside of the current "universe" of poetry that it requires a different classification not utilizing the descriptive "modern."

The answer to that Question, about the need for a new articulation of a category, itself presents another embedded definitional conundrum: even if these works indeed fall outside of "modern poetry," does that mean that the new classification should be articulated as poetry "in a parallel universe"? Perhaps some other categorical definition would be more informative and less arbitrary.

However, since I have chosen not to argue with the wording of the Question, as derived from the language chosen by the curator of the exhibit at the Paris Museum of Modern Art, I think I owe you at least an inkling as to what a "parallel universe" entails.

And this "inkling" proves to be complex beyond easy analysis. Below is a sampler of thoughts about what a parallel universe is or how it would function, derived anecdotally from film, fiction, poetry and, finally and without warranty of scientific exactitude, that ever-popular genre we call quantum physics.

If you pay attention, you learn that our collective awareness is abuzz with various theories of alternative universes. Part of the reason for the buzz is the nascent state of metaverses, electronic worlds that produce gaming, advertising opportunities, and the counter-intuitive practice of purchasing digital merchandise to be worn by or used by avatars in an artificial electronic space.

But part is driven by the contemplation of possible different universes in real time; or is it real space, if there is a difference? In the November 7, 2022 issue of *The New Yorker,* an article entitled "The Never-Ending Story" explores the history of the concept of different universes and the analogous current excitement about multiverses, tracing a tortuous path from early literary discussion to graphic novels to current cinema.

The article does not do a deep dive into film and fiction, by the way; it omits my favorite example the classic Stephen King/Peter Straub novel *The Talisman* (1984) where the principal character flips between realities with aplomb. Not to mention the charming movie *About Time* which is more akin to the slightly analogous possibility of time travel (there the theory is that everything now and in the future already now and forever exists and you can just drop by like Michael J. Foxx in *Back to the Future*).

And I have been waiting in vain for *The House on the Strand* by Daphne du Maurier to be made into a movie, where the protagonist becomes addicted to the drama of the Middle Ages to his ultimate detriment.

To get a flavor for how confusing it might be if there

were in fact various universes running in parallel, view the movie *Everything Everywhere All at Once* (mentioned in *The New Yorker* article). The principal character moves smoothly from her laundromat to kung fu master, although she shows up also in numerous less salutary situations as the universes flip as if riffling a deck of cards.

I am reminded of the oft-cited theory in quantum mechanics revolving around Schrodinger's cat. This poor animal is in a sealed chamber and is at risk of death if, and only if, a random device is triggered. While the chamber is sealed, we do not know whether the cat is alive or dead, so the parallel universe tells us the cat is both alive and dead. When the chamber is opened, we have either a live animal or, in the alternative, according to Ian McEwan, in his 2022 tour-de-force *Lessons*, "an animal dead in a universe inaccessible to the owner or her cat." Are we locked in a circular semantic quibble? Well, according to McEwan: "By extension, the world divides at every conceivable moment into an infinitude of invisible possibilities." (Is it not surprising that these observations appear in a book tracing the life arc of a failed minor poet?)

At risk of doing more harm than good, I now reference famous physicist Michi Kaku who, in his book *Parallel Worlds*, explains that according to quantum theory there is some probability of every conceivable event. "Electrons, in fact, regularly dematerialize and find themselves on the other side of walls… [T]he reason why molecules are stable and the universe does not disintegrate is that electrons can be in many places at the same time. But if electrons can exist in parallel states, then why can't the universe?… Once we introduce the possibility of applying the quantum principle to the universe, we are forced to consider parallel universes."

I trust that Professor Kaku's explanation makes it all clear, particularly as relating to poetry…

Finally, I loved the novel *The French Lieutenant's Woman* by John Fowles, as well as the stunningly successful film of the same name. Reading the novel, the story seems to end with a couple of hundred pages remaining and, confused, you turn to the next page and find yourself back in time and the story then continues on a completely different track. (The film solves this jarring plot shift of parallel universes by setting the story during the making of the film itself, and the two lovers end together in the film-within-the film, while the actors themselves do not end so salubriously in real life.)

None of the literature or film iterations seem to consider the eschatological ramifications of the possible existence of multiple universes in real time. If there are multiple realities, one might think that no decisions need be made, ever, as all possibilities now and forever will co-exist no matter what we do. Would this lead to chaos, or immorality, or the abandonment of the idea of heaven, as good and evil are forever equally present? Or, is this confusion non-existent, in that the "I" for each of us can be perceived only within each separate universe of which that "I" is aware, unconfused by chaos or anomaly roiling in one or even an infinite number of parallel realities—after all, each other universe is occupied only by a distinct avatar of ourselves.

OTHER TITLES

POETRY

Messing Around with Words

Rail Head

Obligatory COVID Chapbook

Laertes in America – Collected Poetry 2018–2020

Burn-Out

PROSE

Noir Ain't the Half of It

    A collection of short stories

The Event

    A novel

You may follow the author, and share your thoughts, by visiting his literary blog site:

https://smhonigauthor.com